Baptism Under Fire

The Journey of a Black Man

Volume 1

by

Shaheem L Dantzler M.D.

DORRANCE
PUBLISHING CO
EST. 1920
PITTSBURGH, PENNSYLVANIA 15238

Dorrance Publishing Co
585 Alpha Drive
Pittsburgh, PA 15238
Visit our website at www.dorrancebookstore.com

ISBN: 978-1-6393-7447-2
eISBN: 978-1-6393-7508-0

It has truly been an journey this past two years to say the least There's been good times, bad times, great memories and flat out depressing moments in time combined with some of the happiest, impactful lessons I've learned in this lifetime. I could have never made it through the fire pits of these tumultuous trails and tribulations without two of the most captivating Women I have ever had the pleasure of having in my life. Both women playing two totally different roles in my life at the time, but still we all had the same goal in mind. The mission was keeping me grounded and happy throughout my depressions , and self- petty , being sure to steer me clear of an unscrupulous characters/situations as well as my own personal behaviors. Always fixing my crown, as a reminder that I am King, I appreciate you both My Oracle And Soul Sistah Lezlee Bee and My Chewie the one who helped me Reach my next level. I love you, I appreciate you, most people are temporary but you two magnificent black Queens will live in my heart forever.

Sincerely, yours

Shaheem Dantzler M.D

Entering different gateways throughout life can be as mellifluous as a violinist hitting each note, ever so harmoniously. In other phases, life can be as deleterious as a building falling on you. These feelings of happiness and pain alter throughout the different phases of your life. Childhood, teen years, and adulthood all different but yet so very significant, in the parts each phase plays in your life. Like a Grandmaster playing chess, planning each move three steps ahead regardless of the move he or she has to make right in front of them. From bad into good, fear into Courage, pain into growth and healing, each feeling being transformed into wisdom. These are the daily battles we face from birth until death, from sun up to sundown. It's a never ending story and you are the Author, the Narrator, the Main Character and the Publicist, shit, you're the whole damn book if you ask me. Be mindful that no matter how we walk into these gateways, we'll always come out on the other end different then the way you walked in. So like a Grandmaster think three steps ahead while also still focusing on the move at hand. Protect the King and value the Queen, and the story of your life can be a bestseller just like mines. Peace.

11:11

Before it's in your mind, it has to be in your heart first. They say they love you but they barely know you, if you're goin' to bet on someone, always bet on yourself. Create peace through understanding, if the world isn't playing fair you shouldn't be playing fair either. Realizing that some disconnections will save your life, understanding and valuing those lessons will be difficult. Accepting the world's many teachings in its totality will prove to be an everlasting asset in your lifetime. Life is not something that you are supposed to control, it is something you are supposed to share with the world, like a scintillating sun, warm the souls of others with your love. Show balance, show consistency, provide loyalty, simulate trust and worth at its highest levels. Don't be afraid to be the good guy/girl often mistaken as the weak, when in fact they're the most strongest of us all. Fuel your fire with the need to be better than the sum of all your fears, no petty parties, no regrets, no sad faces, just simply be your bighearted self. It's a gift to the world whether it's received or not in its fullest glory. The lives you will touch, the hearts you will fix, will be left with your love residue, like gunpowder at a shooting range, it's everywhere. Aim high and reach for the stars just so u can grab the moon. From one big heart to another, let's heal the broken hearts of world with our iridescent love. We have more than enough pieces to go around, it only takes one heart to fix the next, always remember that.

Heartland

I write with a pen connected directly to my heart all the things that I've experienced and witnessed throughout the years of a unique lifestyle. My heart riding my brainwaves like a Hawaiian surfer on a hot sunny day, Aloha. As my life story is told in written form, the world connected directly to my pen all my flaws, my trials and tribulations, my vibrant love life and tumultuous breakups. I'm excited to see how the world will get to experience me and view my eccentric way of thinking. Prepared to be judged in one way or another, but really deep down inside I couldn't care less. The opinions of others simply pass through my mind, like sand running out of my hand, can't get a grip. The pen hits the paper with a purpose, a detailed dossier is the money, and drugs finished product. 31 chapters of passion, hate, friendships, love, family, violence, adventures and ideologies. Can't forget sex, money, and drugs (LOL). I couldn't be more excited, as my life story is being told to the masses in written form. The story of my life matches the title of the book down to the letter, can you guess what the title of the book is? I wonder if they will make a movie about me.

Pen to Paper

As a black man as a black father, as a black son, friend and brother. It is extremely important to have a woman who can be that sanctuary where you're able to be vulnerable, scared, afraid, and any other emotions you can think of. Something so rare only a few men have actually obtained a partner to achieve this beautiful fulling attainment. Me, myself have struggled to maintain my sanctuary at times for one reason or another fear, doubt, or just feeling not worthy of love. Each and every time I've gone through these counterproductive, self-destructive behavioral mishaps. I've been lucky enough to have looked up and she's there every time with her hand to pull me back into our sanctuary. No matter how much I may have just hurt her, for that I take a strong look in the mirror and 1 remind myself that I've found one of the rarest treasures known in the world! Even the most experienced treasure hunters have not been able to acquire it. She holds value in my life like no other, my future, my love, it belongs to her. It has always been her and will always be her. For she is my only reason to believe in true love, I appreciate you.

Hey, I Need You

If I could choose one word to describe our relationship, it would be enigmatic. If I had to break down the aesthetics of our love into a fraction of just a few words it would be, pure, fulfilling, rare, absolutely elegant, can't forget strong, impregnable, just downright incredible. If I had to sum up this past year with you, it would go as such, wonderful, scary, exciting, healing, some would even argue therapeutic. From our past heartbreaks and lessons I've learned, that me and you have been loved by few, hated by few but very few have been ambivalent about us. To me that speaks volumes, we have turned a causal relationship into a truly divine, life-changing, soul-bending, inviolable love. I will be forever grateful to you for as long as I live.

On this day I would like to say thank you, for helping this young black boy understand the man, the king he had growing inside of him. Transcending love and energy, the passion and support that has allowed us to be transmuted into our most divine forms. Black love, damn, it looks good on us. I love you.

Arcane

She makes my heart melt like ice cream on a hot summer day

She brings me joy as if I was a kid in a candy store

She provides mental and physical therapy, you would think she was a doctor (lol)

She loves at such a high propensity, it's impossible to keep her off my mind, I have to have her

She makes me feel safe as if her heart is a fortress around mines

She is a constant reminder that there is still good in this world

If she Eva ask how I feel about her, I would simply say my love for her is an eternal blaze impossible to put out.

Still her love is divine and unmatched, truly rare in every aspect of the world, lucky me!!!

Birds Flying High

Who am I? A loving father, a brother, a support system and friend to many, a proud black man. Who am I ? A monster, a savage, maybe I am a coward, the jury is still out. I take a step back to look into this man's history from an outside view. He's loved and he's been hurt at times, even disappointed by the ones he loved most. Still his love for everyone never waivers, instead he starts to hate himself and questions is everyone better off without him, thoughts of suicide run rampant through his head. Unappreciated, feeling inadequate and just completely decimated at times. It's up to him to save himself, a light goes off in his soul... he's greatest prizes are his children and only they can rescue him from the dark. Who am I? I've saved more lives than have taken, does that make me a good person or an evil man? My ability to give love so effortlessly and on the other hand ripping it away without batting an eye knowing the catastrophic damage it may cause. Am 1 a monster, a savage, maybe I am something different, a grey area. Who do I, good man in this cold world that demands you to be volatile at times, especially want to be? A loving father, a husband, a family man. I want to be as an unapologetic black man. Who am I and who I want to be? Still unknown, still undecided!

Me

It's a battlefield goin' on within me, grenades goin' off, bullets flying from left to right. Gunpowder fogs the air, thick, and smells of death. I can see two silhouettes as the fog starts to dissipate. Chills shoot up my spine, the two silhouettes are now clear. It's Shaheem, my true divine self, and on the other side it's Shyse, my alter ego with that bloodthirsty look in his eyes. The battle within me rages on, I can't keep putting myself in a box, I can't allow Shyse to control everything as he tries to protect Shaheem. I can't continue to allow someone to decide what I can or cannot do. I have to fight myself, I cannot fight the evolution of my divine being anymore. Allowing people to hurt me and acting like nothing happened would be putting myself in a box, blocking my blessings because I want to act one way when I know I should be acting another way. I must stop putting myself in a box, the battle within myself must come to an end. I surrender, I surrender to the divine beings who watch over me, I surrender to myself and allow this change to take place, it's divine timing. I surrender to love, the thing I crave most in this world, I think Shaheem and Shyse would agree. No more boxes, no more fighting, no more pain, just the journey into, divinity, love and tranquility!

Shaheem vs. Shyse

A dog on a leash not fully free and at the same time bonding by love of its owner. How is its freedom define, which opinion is the right one. Free to love, free to roam the world with no worries of apprehension or harm, free to piss on every fire hydrant without judgment. I believe the dog and its owner must have trust love 'n loyalty for one another in order for the dog to fully free leash or not. A walk through the park can seem like a lifetime to dog on a leash if they have the right partner.

Man's Best Friend

As he looks deep into her palace, the sweet aroma of golden silk honey hits his nose!! He can immediately taste her on the tip of his tongue. Soft kisses to the neck and inner thigh, she replies, "Fucc me," [illegible] a look in her eye dat would shake the soul of the devil.

His dick stands at attention, strong, black 'n long. As he thrust his manhood into the sweet honey palace, as it is drenched in heated passion 'n lust as she climaxes with back-to-back orgasms.

Her pussy wet 'n dripping, his dick coded with his queen's sweet nectar, he sprints to the finish line as she helps him along, screaming, "Fuck me, fuck me!!! Fill me up, Daddy …." They climax simultaneously as they snatch each other's souls! Fully satisfied, he seals it with a kiss to the forehead as he says, "I love you, give me a minute and I'll fuck you again."

Drip

Passionate, driven, excited. These are the thoughts that come to mind as I take on the next chapter in my life. I have a beautiful, intelligent black woman in my life. My kids are growing right in front of my eyes, priceless moments of pride and joy. Education, introductions, values, principles that must be taught and received to breed success. I don't fear failure, I will pursue my happiness no matter the cost. Being right with myself will allow me the wherewithal to share it with the ones hold most dear. My queen, my kids, my family. I am the absence of fear, I am the light that shines in the dark, as well as the light who can breed darkness with simple flick of the switch. Happiness is what I want and success is what I need. More importantly I want my kids, my queen, my family to be proud of me. Now that is the ultimate inebriation of feelings and emotions driven by love and passion. Excited to see what's next!

Uphill Climb

I've meet a woman, and instantly I felt a connection I've Neva experienced before, my mind is blown, my heart is confused as I try to come to grips with this amazing yet new scary feeling. I start to question everything I thought I've known about love, about myself as a man. Damn, I feel liberated when I am with her, she's a freedom fighter and my heart is the revolution. I feel safe, more confident, I feel like a man greater than the sum of all his fears! Who is this amazing black woman, who is this stranger who has redefined love in the deepest pits of my soul. As she literally breathes light into me, I am thankful, truly in complete bliss. The ultimate high, nothing else can compare to the way she's changed my life. That block of ice that used to be my heart is now a home for love and appreciation. If I could only tell her in a few words how I felt. I would tell her, she's a divine being, she's everything good about this world, she has recused me from a path of self-destruction. I call her God, the black woman is the only one for me. Fragile, vulnerable, at times weak minded! She doesn't bat an eye, instead she reinforces that I am a king, a god, a black man. I am actually where 1 am supposed to be with the love of my life! The black woman.

Reflection

As I look deep into my soul, I can feel the pain and hurt of a broken heart, the odor of disappointment fills the room. As I look deeper I see a coward, a failure. I tell myself these things as a constant reminder to always fight!! No matter what the cost. Looking past the mirror, past my soul, I take a look into my heart and there is what has always been there, a man who wants to be greater than the sum of all his fears!! A man who wants to be loved and understood as well as be able to love and understand without fear of a broken heart.

One day I hope to find my true self, when that day comes I will embrace him wit open arms.

I'll tell him am proud of you, black man!!

Courage under Fire

A beautiful flower has blossomed, stems strong 'n stern, petals smooth and delicate, smells of a fresh summer breeze as I put my nose to it.

Roots deeply implanted into the earth, pumping into life into the world.

This beautiful flower that has blossomed so vibrantly started off a seed among other seeds, but somehow comes out different, comes out perfect!!! Not perfect in the sense of flawlessness but in the ability to overcome and adapt to any weather!

Hot summer days, stifling heat

Brutal winters, frozen tundras, rainy spring days.

As this flower grows from a seed to a stem into one of the most beautiful things on earth!! I look back from the start of its journey. I take a second to appreciate the strength and beauty of it all, but more importantly the growth

This beautiful flower, I call her Johnnie Lee

Pink Petals

My every thought of her lights the flame inside of me. Our love burns bright and beautiful like a bad bitch on a hot summer's day. When I think of her I realize my heart and my mind are in sync, she's perfect for me!! Everything I've ever dreamed of has come true. I feel like a kind. She makes sure to remind me daily.

Fast forward to the future, am still heavy on her body, my love still as deep and patient as it's Eva been. My gray hairs matching hers (lol), cups if water by the bedside for our dentures. She has my heart 'n I have hers until the end of time. When I think of her, she's the love I noe I want and deserve, if I am lucky enough I can make her just as happy as she makes me.

Midnight Blue

Pure unadulterated love, dat feeling you've always wanted since you was a lil' girl

Am sure it's times when I give you butterflies and you feel like dat girl all ova again, excited and scared. At the same time, still driving head first, that excitement, the mysteriously dope energy, it's all one

You feel it every time I touch you, from ur head to ur toes. At dat moment it's clear and you realize this is the first time you've ever really been in love

Pure Madness

All I ever wanted was to be a part of your heart and for us to be together, and Neva part

In your eyes I see our present, our future and past, by the way you look at me I know we will last

My heart feeds off of your, my soul is complete when ur by my side and it hurts to see you leave.

As I wait anxiously for ur return, here you are walking towards me, in complete bliss as you bless my presence. My queen is back in her castle

I hope that one day you'll come to realize, how perfect you are when seen through my eyes.

Perfection in My Heart

A chair is still a chair, even if it's no one sitting there. Your eyes are a gateway into who u are at your core, the deepest part of the soul. 75 percent of the human body is made up of water and like a raging river or a calming ocean, the water stores and hold memories. All the fears you have, all the love you give, your core principles, every life-changing moment you have, good and bad. Constantly flowing through you, waiting for the day it's needed as a reflection of growth or stagnant behavior. Like a gentle breeze running across your face, you can feel it, you can smell it, but you can touch it, but we know it's there, it's real. I take a seat in an empty chair as I look outwards to appreciate the view, I can see people walking, talking, enjoying the scenery of the outdoors, it's music to my ears. I catch sight of a school of ducklings and their mother crossing the road into the pond, I'm reminded of my little ones, my kids, my heart, my lifeline. It's truly a beautiful sight to witness and capture with a simple snap of my camera, an instant memory stored in the body of water I have flowing through me, it's been a good day, one to remember.

8 Ducks and a Man

Annihilation, trust the timing of your life. Know that everything happens exactly the way it is supposed to happen. Granted we all miss an opportunity or two, we may have overlooked a few blessings, not being cognizant of the path put before us. No regrets, no re-deals, no water works, pick your head up and play the cards you have in your hands. Think outside the box, make decisions based off of your confidence and abilities, not your fears and self-limitations. Be that strong, unmovable, ready to annihilate everything in its path walking, talking freight train that u often daydream about. Ambassador of yourself, king/queen of your own castle, mentally and physically, be savory, a helping hand to those who look like and resemble you inside and out. This mindset, this lifestyle can and at times will take a toll on you, no doubt about it. Always remember why we was put here on this earth, not for our own selfish needs and wants but to make the world a better place in its entirety. Working hard on yourself to help yourself and therefore being able to help others, leading up into each one. Teach one each one reach one, causing a chain reaction of events that will inspire a nation. To do better, as well as to be better, think smarter, work smarter, more efficient in every aspect of life, including our personal encounters with the people who look like us. Love one another, trust one another, and the most important thing, respect everything that u can't see in the dark. We control the light and the dark with just the flip of a switch. Don't undermine your generosity and never underestimate your own power individually and as a unit, bend but don't break, the world needs you.

BLK

She fucks my soul, she fellatios my mind. Her pussy throbbing my dick, pounding like a heat-seeking missile ready to explode in that pussy!! Her orgasms gives off the intensity of two honeybees fighting for the last drop of honey. It's that good, last man standing, last dick swinging. I need to have her, I want to have her inside 'n out, on the bed or on the table, slap that ass and choke the shit outta her, mmm. My God, this woman is divine and am addicted to her pussy, her soul, her mind, her womanhood. Spit in her pussy 'n suck it back out while she shouts out, "Daddy, damn," I respond wit silence, I just start to eat her assty, her toes damn near bend backwards. Again she shouts out, "Daddy, Daddy," I know l got her! I flip her over as I take a deep dive into her hive, almost simultaneously she orgasms all over the place. I continue to swim in her pussy, loving every second of it as I stare down and look deep into her eyes, past her membrane and into her soul! We both climax at the same time, you can hear a pin drop as our energy electrifies the room. We lay down and hold each other tight 'n it ends wit kiss on the forehead and I love you, Queen!

Pounding the Pavement

As she lays there resting peacefully after a long day, I take a moment to reflect and appreciate the effort and grace put on display daily by this woman, she's a goddess.

It's only right I try to ingratiate myself into the deepest blood vessels In her heart. I need to embody her soul with mines, the intention is to become one divine being.

I fade into a deep trance, getting lost in my heart, putting my mind and foresight to the test.. I envision our lives together and it's nothing less than sensational!! Endless happiness, international trips across the seas, an occasional adventure from time to time just to keep her on her toes (lol). Eventually family ties, generational wealth, money wise as well as love wise.

As she lays, I can feel her breath in love and breath out hate, strong and wise, she is truly. One of a kind, the rarest breed of rare, the black woman!!! I am a man possessed by love, I say this without Equivocation. She's perfect for me, she breaths out I breath in, she steps left, I step right, she jumps, I land, to put it simply we are one!!!

View from the Belvedere

Death has fallen upon me, I can't shake the Grim Reaper, he's always after me. Directly or indirectly he has the same effect on my soul. I'm scared, I'm frightened, constantly looking for the courage to face that unavoidable demon called death. I feel the chills as he walks alongside me daily, I can run but it's proven futile as he will always catch up to me. I must stay one step ahead of this entity called death. Must fight fire with fire if I hope to survive. Death on my mind, pain in my heart, the darkness is upon me, I must be reborn if I hope to survive! A double-edged axe is the weapon of my choice. The trap is set, it's time to kill, time to dismantle and destroy the foundation that gives death this power over me. I swing my axe ferociously. I am a man possessed, full of hatred, fear, pride, thought that should Neva be spoken out loud, I swing right, I swing left, blood splatter one way, his head flying the other way: instantly I can feel my skin shed, I am newborn, I am a vessel of light. The darkness will never win!!

Death in the Air

I thought I had more time with you, I thought I would have more Thanksgivings to spend with you, all the family there eating good and enjoying our time with the queen of family. I remember the smell of breakfast in the morning, the taste of those grits, mmm, still to this day unmatched. I have vivid memories of store runs and off course those walks to the post office. Crossing the streets waiting for the lights to turn green as you grab my hand SO tight, I used to hate that as

young kid but as a grown man wish I could feel that kung fu grip, that sense of protection, I miss you playing Smokey Robinson those Sunday mornings, and those damn stories throughout the week, *All My Children, General Hospital, The Young and the Restless,* I'm thankful for my time with you, still it will never be enough, I need you, I wish you was here with me to celebrate my growth, see the man I've become. Hold your great-grandkids, meeting and loving my future with JL. So far away, damm, I really miss you, I am hurting, I am angry, life isn't the same without you. I just wanna honor your memory, was always a handful and you never loved me less truly unconditionally love. I value every ass whopping you gave me with that damn shoe you kept by your bedside. I long to hear your voice again, Ms. Annie Tartt, see your beautiful smile and off course taste those grits drizzled in butter, mmm, I love it, I thought I had more time, I wish I had more time. Until I see you again, your love will pump through my soul and I will breathe life into everything I touch, knowing that you're looking down on me proud. I can hear you now. It brings tears to my eyes and joy to my heart, Grandma. I know you up there in heaven with your favorite, Kobe, lol you loved u some Kobe. I love you, Grandma, see you soon, your one only Booda!

A Letter to My Grandma

The walls around me are closing in, I start to panic, every breath more heavy than the last. I can smell my own fear, it reeks of disappointment and countless failures. Not deserving of anything love, success, a simple allocate of approval. I start to contemplate a plan that will be conducive to my next plan of action. Every second matters as the walls continue to close around me. I am frozen, I can't think, my respiratory system starts to fail, being ripped out of my control just like everything else. Deep breaths, strong prayers to the innermost intimate places in my spirit, screaming for help! I hear a voice: "Shake off that fear, throw the tears and miscellaneous heartbreaks to the side. Ease your mind of the negative thoughts, free your heart of the burden of the unknown, let your hands free to help others without the feelings of the inevitable disappointment. Simply just look up as the walls close around you, you'll see the daylight. Your way out will always be up, don't forget that. We all have a destiny when it starts to get vigorous, just take a look up and you'll find you way out!!!"

Unknown

I can't sleep, my mind racing think about what's my next big step? Accumulating happiness and wealth in my life, that's the ultimate goal. Not for me, but for these three beautiful little girls that lay in the bed next to me. Bittersweet it is, on one hand I am filled with happiness and joy. I love my girls. It's my job to raise these young ladies to be queens that are more than just the sums of their parts and looks. They have to be intelligent, clever, respectable, trustworthy in a world that will corrupt you and rip out your soul at the drop of a hat. That's the fun part. I look at them wit excitement on my face as they all lay sleeping gracefully. All facing me like one moment stuck in time, a vivid memory that the universe felt I had to see! It's priceless, it's beautiful. The part that sucks is why are all four of us sleeping on a full-size futon? It hits me hard like an iron worker using a sledgehammer, and I am the bolt. I'm failing which is something that I am used to, but not this time, I have to do one thing right in my life. I must dig deep into every neuron and synapse in me to provide my little ladies with the tools to not only survive but to conquer this world. Graduations, career promotions, motherhood, marriage, even their first little crushes, I need to be there. I want to be there to laugh and to cry with my girls if that is the support they need at the time. I am their dad, I am their superhero and they are my lifeline, my three little girls.

Three Girls Raising a King

I hate her, I hate the impact she has on my soul as well as my heart. I feel hopeless, weighted down by my infatuation with finding love. My heart shattered and broken multiple ways by multiple babes, I wanna run, I wanna hide, I start to think maybe I am addicted to the hurt and pain of love. I start to think the pain is all I deserve, no love, no companionship, just hat tricks and a sleight of hands. I look deep within myself begging for answers, possibly some guidance, I hear nothing! My soul is an empty pit. There's only room for pain, hurt, and disappointment, My mind tries to speak to my heart like what the hell is goin' on! My heart responds I love her, if I have to hurt for her then I will, pain is my second nature. My appetite for love is

unattainable, unreachable, limitless. Still I have the urge to try, it's right in front of me still, I can't reach. The hate I have for her is really uncontrollable Love, I'll stop at nothing to have it!

Hate

Pain, torture, blood spattered and head decapitations, just a few of many dark thoughts I have. At times I'd like to torture someone and enjoy every last breath they take. The life that they are desperately fighting to survive for. Not sure if it's the power I yearn for or is it the simple fact I enjoy pain 'n violence. Should I waterboard them, maybe food deprivation or my personal favorite chopping of limbs. Gruesome and beautiful in my darkest thoughts, it's art to me. The patients, the steady hands it takes to remove and repair the wicked. I question my sanity, I wonder do other people think this way. I wanna bask in the pain and swim in the blood-filled bath of desperation, fear, and the inevitable. I envy the serial killers of this world, the Jefferys, the Teds, the B.T.K.s of the world. Not for the actual crimes but their ability to do the unbelievable, most volatile, demeaning disgraceful things and not think twice about it. Go home and eat a steak, go to bed in peace with head in my fridge next to the lemonade. I am a monster in my darkest thoughts! Fear the day the light stops shining in me!

Dark Water

I never would have made it, had it not been for you. You'd just breathe life into me without effort whenever we was near. Your energy, your charisma, the gravitational pull you had on me and everyone around you, is nothing less than a godsend. Much more than just a person, you was a life, would have never made it without you. I remember going, all the love in the world to give without question, damn experience, a journey inside and out save me. Three days of captivity (lol) filled with, knew I had to get next to you for only your energy could truly through the toughest time in my life, adventure, women and cab rides across town from Harlem to the Bronx, for the shop back to the crib. You are my big brother and I'll never forget how u saved my life without even realizing what u was doing. Which was providing a sanctuary for a broken man, I love you the most, he would always say to me and everyone else in arm's reach (lol). Those who had the privilege to call him a friend/family where truly loved by one of the great ones, loved unmatched and never undervalued. I never would have made it without you, big bro. Thank you!!!

Lsk

I'm not going to say goodbye, I'd rather think about the years and good times we spent together. Our last conversation, me texting you, wishing you Happy Mother's Day and you replying thanks, Bro, wit a heart emoji, damn, I'm devastated. My Tay Tay, my heart, my sister, damn, gone way be4 your time. I never thought I would be saying these words of pain and frustration again so soon. So suddenly, so fast, the sweetest little 22-year-old, GONE, damn, thing gone, stripped away from my life. All I can do is scream and ask God why? Why the ones I hold so dear to my heart? Why are you taking them at such a rapid pace, God? I haven't even begun to heal from my last lost and now this. I can't take it, I am literally on the edge, I'm hurting, I'm scared, I wanna scorch the earth, I am so fucking angry. I just wanna fucking know why them, why now? And who is next? Is it me? A mother without her daughter, a son without his mother, a big brother without his little sister, and the world without one of its most beautiful angels, FUCK. I'll see you in a minute, Tay Tay, 1 love you, sis, hold me a seat next to God, I have some questions that need answering.

My Tay Tay

Like the headless horseman, I ravage through the villages cutting off heads, hoping to find myself. As vicious blows, the heads fly clean off. Like I methodically chop these heads off, with a strong surgeon in the operating room, I am precise, my hands are steady, as my mind formulates a plan to recreate my identity, my principles, and my ideologies, but the soul remains the same, warm, welcoming, pure. Some would call me a headless, heartless horseman from hell, as I continue growing my collection of heads. Others would call as I try to put back and replace the pieces of a broken man, me a mad scientist, Dr. Frankenstein, crazy and insane soon to be reborn again. I take the process of a new me, glorified look at my collection of heads as I being to start a beautiful rebirth, it shall be. I begin to notice something, interesting souls, a slight smile runs across my face as I shuffle through my collection of heads and unkept followed by a villainous outburst of laughter. I put the heads in a line on the table and they all look the same, slight differences but nonetheless the same. I recognize their faces and their ideologies, from their own perspectives. Only past life, they are reincarnations of me all different in the soul remains the same from these countless decapitations, it's the urge to continuously be reborn, recreated, improved. It's the mad scientist inside me, the sword-wielding horsemen from hell inside of me, perfect in the proverbial sense, and not what society deems as perfect. Perfect, just simply being the best version of myself I know I can be. I've chosen to put forth together to make a perfect creation. Not a head, now the operation can begin, the mad scientist flips the switch, lightning strikes lifeless specimen, and on, the ground rumbling like a stampede of wild bulls, and the sky is lit up like the Fourth of July. Sparks fly everywhere, the lights flicker off excitement and achievement as the lifeless specimen wakes from a dormant sleep. The energy in the operating room is filled with the doctor screams, "He's alive, he's alive, he's beautiful." The patient slowly opens his eyes and takes a good look at himself, then he looks at his creators ready to speak his first words. They wait to hear what he will say, you can feel the anticipations in the room, it's a sharp as a knife cutting through butter. The man looks and says, "Our work isn't done, gentleman, keep collecting heads, this one will suffice for now!"

The Legend of a Black Man

Only I can stand the rain, can get love or I can shed blood, only I can control the psychological view of the world, the called proverbial way of living, only I can define who I am inside and out, a good man or a monster hell bent on pain, violence and death. Like a lost child looking for his parents, confused, hurt, devastated, no sense of direction, completely destroyed. Only I can stop the pain as I stand in the rain soaked from head to toe, my clothes heavily weighing me down. As the inner voice in my soul struggles to react out to my mind 'n heart, take a few deep breaths as I close my eyes, let the rain wash away, all my fear, all my hesitation, all my doubts, it's rejuvenating. My pride is intact, my heart is racing and pure, my mind is as clear as a sheet of fog disappearing from the sky. It's all good, it's all right, I can stand the rain, I am the rain, I am self, mind, body and soul. I can rain water or I can rain fire A blood, sweat and tears. I can stand the rain

Clear Skies

When a Woman Loves

It's the ultimate gift from the universe

She can instantly turn a bad day good with her illuminating smile

She'll dedicate her life and time to you without question

Her sweet nectar flows naturally as she soaks the sheets and your manhood

She fears only the loss of pure love

She becomes as majestic and elegant as a god!! strong and wise like an elephant

She brings confidence and ambition into a relationship embellished wit kisses and great memories

When a woman loves, keep her floating on air in a constant state of bliss. Keep her wet and craving for more.

When a woman loves, you'll become whole, you'll become one. You'll witness the true meaning of Love

When a Woman Loves

From the moment i laid my eyes on her, I knew my soul would be dissatisfied if I couldn't have her.

I want to understand her more than she understands herself. If I can love her demons, her pain, her joy, than I myself can achieve complete happiness.

The deep dive begins, as I pull back the layers, it's so much to learn and appreciate. she's strong full of hope and passion, even though on the inside she's scared to death to be disappointed by love again!! Yet she continues to take those chances, she's a warrior, there's no doubt about it.

The electric energy that inhabits our souls can be seen from miles away.

It's ferocious, its beautiful, truly a sight to see. The good, the bad, the illumination of light and spirit.

To understand her is to understand her worth at its highest level. She deserves the world, not because she's perfect but for her unequivocal ability to love, despite countless disappointments that was not warranted. It should have broken her, and still she raises to the occasion without hesitation, she's a goddess in my eyes.

As i resurface from my journey into her mind, body, and soul. I've come to the realization to understand her completely you must understand yourself. It won't work if you're giving 75 percent and she's giving 100. With her you have to embody your own demons, pains, and joys, to fully understand as well as respect the love she possesses.

Let her know you see her daily, let her know she's understood, tell her every day that she's safe. Let her know love is here and it's not goin' anywhere. Kiss her on the forehead and tell her she's god in your eyes.

Understanding her is a journey I would go on over and over, to understand her is to understand love

B.W.O. (Black Women Only)

Creations, manifestations, the rebirth of a black man. As I look at the glass half full I'm reminded that it's not what's in the glass that matters, but more so what the glass is made out of. Throughout my life and daily struggles I find true meaning in the word love as well as

life in its entirety. The glass is a representation of what has already happened as well as what is to come. No matter how hard life get I will rise like greater appreciation for orchid on a moist sunny day with just a hint of a cool breeze to push me forward as I strive for immortality. A father thinks. A deity in my purest form, one day I hope to achieve this mighty feat and all its Divine Glory. Until then I'll hold the crown as king! A strong son, a brother among other dedicated black men in my own rights. Evolution is what I crave, revolution is what I demand and more importantly love is all I need to keep me afloat in this hostile universe. Like a single rose petal in a glass half full, I will not drown.

Glass Half Full

Trust is something that is so easily given, but at the same time it's so hard to get back after you've violated the trust of another person. Given to you as a gift with a sense of pride behind it not to be mistreated or mishandled. It may seem like a small gesture, when in fact it's one of the most incredible gifts a person can give to you, it's priceless, outside of material things. You lie, you hide, and you hurt, selfishly you are expecting that the person who gave u a chunk of themselves to just forgive and forget. It's insane to think that the same gift of trust and love you was given, to be on the same level as was before, after you've mishandled it with no regards whatsoever. You don't deserve it, probably shouldn't have had it to start off with, but still the trust is there to an extent. Not because the person actually trusts you still 100 percent, it's the fact that they wanna think more highly of you, than just a violator of their trust. It's just human nature, no one wants to feel like they made a mistake giving away such a beautiful gift, only for it to be squandered and put to the side like an old toy on Christmas morning. Not caring about the ramifications or repercussions of their own actions, shame. I say that to say this, trust is your gift to give as well as your gift to receive, treat it as such, truly priceless gift. Easily given, nearly impossible to get back after it's broken, never take it for granted. There's no telling if you'll ever get it back after you lose it. It's more than just a gift, it's privilege and a honor to obtain one's trust, treat it as such!!!

Trust No One

Speak light and love into yourself. Don't be afraid to reinvent yourself for the betterment of yourself and the nations you one day hope to build, and yes, that includes a step outside of your proverbial box, analyze and assess the data of the world around you. Archaic way of thinking is obsolete deep dive into self. Bridging those gaps within yourself will help towards a more indestructible foundation. Therefore leading up to the tasks at hand, what is the task I speak of, u ask, is it world domination? Is it the elevation of my race? Is it self-proclaimed excellence? My response is all of the that's your preference. From the moment I wake up until I close my eyes and go to sleep, my mind is a racetrack. The above, in whichever order that's your preference. From the moment I wake up, until I close my eyes and go to sleep, my mind is a racetrack. The Kentucky Derby, Daytona 500, 100-meter dash as I analyze the obstacles, the different opponents, the vigorous landscapes. Always planning steps ahead, trying to figure out how to beat the odds, how to manipulate the system and make it benefit my needs and aspirations. Learning my opponents, their strengths and weaknesses, learning to manipulate myself for the task at hand whether it be mentally or physically, my goal is to be. Before you can start to do the work, you must work on you first. Fixing your views three dimensional in a world where perception means everything. Things, people, and places are from its lowest to highest thoughts, adjusting your mentality when it comes to the societal views of the world in which, deemed to be inadequate or simply just taking up space. Reinvent your general ways of thinking, down to the blueprints of how you give and process information. Speak light and love into yourself, only then can u pass on that gift of balance to others in need of that light and love.

Invention of the Lightbulb

As a grown man i take a look back in time, coming to the realization that the one person i looked up to more than Malcolm X is my dad. Baseball games, basketball games and amusement parks, countless trips to the movies theaters and my personal favorite every weekend at the skating rink (The Key). That man taught me the game, and I take pride into perfecting it. He has shown me the definition of a great father, i was in a privileged position to learn and i soaked it all up like a sponge. From the teachings of Islam to negotiating the world in white America. Having knowledge as well as the understanding on how to use that knowledge is step one, developing the ability to process time,money, and information, that's step two. Put family first and never turn you're back on the people who looks like you, together we are a formidable opponent, step three. He taught me to be a gangster and a gentleman in every aspect of the word, i will always be grateful to my best friend who is also my dad. Having seen most of my friends in single family homes has truly given me a great appreciation for what I had right in arms reach. A king raising a prince I just gotta say thanks dad I appreciate you, live free, die black, father and son for life.

From Son to Father

To the woman of my dreams who has become my reality. I'll start off by saying you are the equivalent of a beautiful sunny day. Hot, fun, wet, full of adventure and excitement, as the day shifts into a warm summer night. I see the stars are out as you gaze into my eyes, the moon shining its light on your alluring personality and prepossessing intellect. My heart racing like a prize horse at the Kentucky Derby. I'm all in, ten toes down, my mission is your love and the prize is your eternal soul and captivating beauty. As this pulchritudinous summer day comes to an end, I realize it's the dead of winter lol and it's cold as hell. But as long as I have you in my life, I can have these beautiful summer days no matter the season. I love you, Chewie, I'll see you at the finish line 10!

Serenity

It's been a long but calm day and I'm in the mood for some soul snatching. I text my queen, "I'm on my way, get the oils and the candles out, it's time for a dick-down massage session." She replies, "Heard you, Daddy, I'm get her warmed up for you!" As I enter the house, the aroma of sweet vanilla and lavender fills the air. She meets me at the door with her sexiest outfit on. Butt-ass naked, mmm, I love it. Grab her ass as I seductively kiss her sweet full lips. I take my clothes off as we walk to the bedroom, rose petals leading up to the bed, and candles lit all over the room. I whisper in her ear, "It's time, beautiful, now get that sexi ass on the bed and lay on ur stomach." She throws her ass in the air on all fours as she slowly begins to lay across the bed. I reach for the oil as I start to give her a deep tissue massage, I can feel her body quiver with every touch of my hands. Lust fills the air, pussy wet and throbbing, I can feel the drips on the tip of my dick as I gently kiss her back from top to bottom. I hear her say, "Daddy, I need u now," as she grabs my dick and places it inside her pussy, fat, dripping 'n warm, mmm & time for the 9th inning. "Hey, Siri, put on the Bedroom playlist," begin stroking and pounding her pussy to the flow of the music. Each stroke more intense than the last, dipping in and out of her pussy, rubbing my dick on her click just for good measure as I flip her on her back. I take a deep look past her eyes and I capture her soul as she soaks the bed coming back to back, her legs shaking profusely. "Whose pussy is it? Who's Daddy?" She can barely speak, eyes rolled to the back of her head, she's in complete bliss. I take a few more strokes as I kiss her lips down to her stomach and on to her honey palace, it's time for snack break. I begin to eat her pussy, she can't take, she tries to push me off 'n lock her legs. I push her hands anyway and grip her inner thighs, as I collect her honey with each lick of my tongue, with each kiss of my lips, it's a river rafting adventure for my mouth. Snack break is over, back to soul snatching, she grabs me and says, "It's my turn," as she hops right on my dick. I'm loving every second of it as she bounces and grinds on my dick, all I can think is damn, she got me, I tell her, "Choke me and spit in my mouth, baby, let's get nasty." Her hands wrapped around my neck, her legs sturdy as she gets on her tippy toes, she's goin' for the home run. I palm her ass, "Yeah, baby, ride that dick, Daddy ready to come!" Her pussy grips my dick and snatches my soul right out of me, as I bathe in her squirt, damn, that was amazing. She lays across my chest soak and wet, with my dick still inside of her, I hold her tight and kiss her forehead, it's been a full-on soul exchange, truly beautiful. I look at her deep in her eyes and ask her who's gonna clean up all these rose petals and blow these candles out (lol). She laughs and says, "You, Daddy, it was your idea" (lol).

Soul Exchange

I wonder if she knows that she has captured the heart of a lion. I wonder to myself, has this man actually been captured, or is he willingly surrendering to the power of love w. different perceptions but still the same outcome. She has captured his heart, not wit violence or manipulation, but with a delicate touch directly to the heart, a passion that burns bright, a beautiful blaze truly, its velocity is endless. The symmetry between the captured and the captor is advantageous, beautiful, refreshing, their love has become an amazing form of art. I humbly come to my conclusion, the man although fearless, strong and clever has no choice but to admire 'n surrender to this woman. A seamless fusion of beauty and intelligence, truly a divine work of art. I deem her priceless, put her on display for the world to see! True art deserves an audience and she deserves king, she deserves love!!

Captured

Every day I need to be next to you, every second of every day I wanna feel your heartbeat next to mines. You're the first person I think about before I go to sleep and the first person I think about when I wake up. Your beautiful soul and big heart is truly unassailable, the way I need you is insanely close to obsession. In fact, the love you give is as pure and natural as breathing in air. Have no say in the matter, obsession is my only choice. I need your love on every level until the day fades away. I'll be sure to always fix your crown daily, you deserve it. Loving you, healing with you, growing with you. I am a man on a mission hell bent on purifying my obsession for you and turning it into a passionate creation of loyalty, honor, respect and balance. But most importantly loving you, the rarest treasure on God's green earth, Q, the Black woman.

Love Phobia

No one controls a strong man's fate. No one controls a wise woman's destiny. A strong man and a wise woman, you say? An interesting, yet a dynamic pairing of the two, I like it, I'm intrigued. If and when these two unique souls meet, I can only imagine the electrifying, pulse-stopping, mind-blowing chain of events that will cause with just a kiss of the lips. Magnificent, beautiful, spectacular, even these eloquent words cannot come close to truly depicting that divine moment, visually or emotionally. It just is! It's been preordained for this love to bless the universe. As they spread love and inspiration to the furthest reaches of space and time. A strong black man, wise black woman. A gift even the gods would appreciate, a gift our fallen ancestors would be proud of. As they watch from above, front-row seats in the sky, filled with joy and pride. The great ancestors can only equate this moment with the disentanglement of their bondage, chains and shackles. That insatiable feeling for freedom and love combined into one, it's a beautiful sight to witness. No one controls a strong black man's fate. No one controls a wise black woman's destiny. Grab your popcorn and get ready to experience the never-ending story of Black Love.

Bet on Black

I've went my whole life without seeing myself for who I truly am. Only the versions I've created and developed over the years, along with the projected. The journey from a young spirited black boy with the world at his disposal, into a grown black man with the image I've held in the eyes of others. Constant uphill battles and gut checks. This journey has had its fair share of wins and losses deep down inside, knowing that it will all worth it on that day when I can look in the mirror and recognize myself, no mask, no different personas, just me, Shaheem. I've been many things over the course of 31 years, it's been an adventure to say the least, definitely dark and scary at times for sure, straight up depression for a long time. Allowing myself to grow and reach out for help has made me a stronger man and a better person. The people I've meet in my life, my loved ones that I've shared my love and pain with, along with the lessons I've learned. I can now reflect on my journey in a healthy, constructive way after finding my balance, my confidence. I take a bow and give thanks to my one true love, the black woman, she's helped me shape my life into one I know she'll be proud of one, I am a brother, I am a son, a friend to most and day. Will continue to work harder and harder no matter the cost, I can't lose, I won't lose. I am a father, a loved one to many. More importantly I am a beautiful black man with my one true love in my corner. I am still figuring out this thing called "Self." I'm filled with excitement. I feel confident in myself as I look and plan for the future. Knowing myself, loving myself, giving the necessary praise and appreciation to the people who've touched my life during this journey of "Self." I am optimistically looking forward to that day when I can look myself in and be able to answer with pride and tears in my eyes as I reply, "Yes!! I know who is in the mirror," and ask that question, "Do you know who you are...?"

Shaheem, the Real Shaheem

My heart, strong as an ox, my way of thinking methodical and rapid. Effortless to the outside world, although deep down inside I must admit from time to time I feel that cold chill up my spine. My fears and anxiety mixed with a bit of daily reality comes to a head. The pressure and panic rips through my cerebral cortex like a California wildfire. My palms are sweating, my heart beating like a drum at a Pan-African festival. My mind shuts down, body starts to shake, I'm trapped, it's life or death from this point forward. Questions running through my mind, looking for answers like a pop quiz on an unexpected Friday lol. Damn, I have to pull it together, do I abide by their rules? Do I exercise my rights and ideology as I see fit? It's fight or flight, I take a few deep breaths as I close my eyes and call to the ancestors for guidance and strength. I'm reminded about the blood I have coursing through my veins passed down from generation to generation. My African blood is powerful but more importantly unique! Full of endless potential, intelligence, strength, love, empathy. The last question I ask myself is how can what I have inside of me be so strong, so powerful, so valuable, but on the outside my beautiful black melanin is deemed dangerous, replaceable, worth less than a bag of dirt? I take one last deep breath, I open my eyes as I look through my rearview mirror. I am just another black man/woman getting pulled over by the POLICE. Live or die I must fight, not just for me but for the integrity and future of my race. The price of freedom is death and I'm willing to pay that price every time. Are you?

Say Their Names

Basking in the ambience of something new, like trying vegan food for the first time. It looks good, smells good but you're not sure or how you're going to react to something, gonna taste garlic knots, and a side of salad, mmm, the second it buds I'm instantly enamored, filled with excitement and fatty and I crave new things, new places, new people r refreshing, so mind blowing, extremely interesting she is. As I pull back the layers of this succulent lasagna understand her more, I can taste the love and energy 5 creations. If I'm lucky I'll have some vegan desserts and chocolate chip chocolates, cupcakes. Mmm, I can almost taste it now, the food that is, her mind, her body, her intellect placed in one creation after another. Damn, I'm hungry for her next creation with my fork and spoon or maybe the hands, that way I can lick them clean. Basking in some such a good feeling.

Tasty Eats

Reprogramming the motherboard you call a brain. Being able to identify the difference between the guilty and the innocent is a rigorous task, if I am being honest. The worst things, places, and people are usually attached to something or someone beautiful. In life everything has its pros and cons as well as its emblematic moments good and bad. It's a beautiful thing to start something from start to finish, life is about the journey, not the destination. Navigating your primal instincts step one, identifying your reactions vs. your responses step two live and die by your core principles, step three, wipe your mind clear of the so-called societal norms, step four, step five fill in the blanks, only you know the superlatives that will truly describe you, as well as the description of your journey. Find balance, pack an umbrella in the event of rain, you'll need it.

Five-Step Map

They say the best way to appreciate life is coming close to losing it. The time and people we take for granted, all them running through the city, when you should have been walking enjoying the structures and scenery of the city. The life u live day to day, try to appreciate the here and now, as u aim for the stars don't forget to put value on the clouds. Every day you wake up is another day for you to improve, perfect your craft, appreciate new life and value the old. Metamorphosis an interesting concept, from an egg into a caterpillar, then a pupa into a butterfly, each step just as special as the next, each level teaches you how to grow and then grow again. Surviving life vs. enjoying life is a common topic, racing through life vs. walking through life, perspective vs. prospective. I say whichever one you choose, be sure to slow down just for a second and smile, look up in the sky and let the sun hit your face. Stop and look in the mirror as you tell yourself, "I love you." Find someone special to laugh with, have disagreements with, start a family and a business with. Take a minute to pass down wisdom and knowledge to your children, as well as anyone else in need. Have honor, stand strong by your convictions, be altruistic every chance you get. They say the best way to appreciate life, is coming close to losing it. I say don't wait that long.

Arduous

Hope doesn't hold up a mirror, and let you know it's there. You can't go through life with regret as your only company. It's okay to want something for yourself, it's okay to feel afraid and alone, it's okay to be loved and helped. But if you're afraid I suggest you not be alone and if you're alone it's no time to be afraid. If someone is helping you to accept love, then u should take it. If being in love is allowing you to appreciate help from another, don't take it for granted. You ask, what is the demarcations? When you're being repeatedly defenestrated as you attract the same type of people, just in different variations. The answer is you have to have hope. Hope you have the strength and intelligence to change within yourself. Build strong principles backed up by maintaining boundaries will help with the pain. Hope that you can look past your own ego, hope that pride won't get in the way of logic and reasoning. Hope that fear and regret don't run your life and every decision you make. Hope that you have the ability to apply faith over logic and reasoning when the time comes because it will come, hope that u can tell the difference. Hope that when you've been mentally destroyed, that you have someone in your corner that you can lean on for help and love. Hope that when your heart is broken into pieces, that there will be someone to help piece it back together, stronger, more resilient, more pure. Hope that when you achieve all your dreams, you have someone to celebrate life with, real love is rare and someone having your back forever is even harder to find than love, so hope u can get both out of your life partner. Hope that you can pass on your legacy down to the kids of the future, hope that they won't have to go through half of what u had to endure, in this thing called life. Hope that you can spark the mind of the person who will change the world. Hope, love, fear, help, regrets, pain, being alone, having faith, are just a few things that show up in different forms and at different times in your life, it's no way around it. I hope you have the ability to love through your fears, and pains. I hope that you have help when you are feeling alone. I hope you have faith in yourself, faith that your past regrets won't repeat itself. I hope after reading this you become a better version of yourself, because I've become stronger writing this. I hope that when you look in the mirror, you can see a new hope, I hope you can see yourself.

Hope

This last year has revealed so many things to me. The good, the bad, the abustle ugly, as I continue my path in life I have the urge to be the best version of myself I can be, no more feeling sorry for myself, no more letting others dictate my energy. It's been days when I couldn't even look at myself in the mirror. I'm hurting, I wanna just die some days and leave this place, it's not fair, everyone and everything I love just getting snatched away from me. I'm pissed off, I wanna hurt someone. These are some of the things I go through in my mind on a daily basis. I can love everyone around me without hesitation, but when it comes to loving myself I can't seem to do it and that shit holds me back from achieving all that I can accomplish in this life. I'm strong, I'm tough and weak all at the same time. I could be a beautiful person or I could be a viscous savage animal. It's no telling who will receive what version of me on any given day. I miss my loved ones, they are gone and I'll Neva be able to hold them in my arms again. Just the realization of that is destroying me, I smile, I laugh but it's short lived. My mind, my body dies more and more every time someone is snatched from me. I've reinvented myself over and over, I try to be a better me, I need to be more understanding, more openminded, there is nothing that can stop the tears, the pain, the destruction that's already underway. My kids, my Chewie are the only ones that have kept me sane, without them it's complete darkness. They show me that every day it's light even when everything dark, and something positive in everything negative. I'm afraid, I can't lose my grip on reality, I can't lose them. Dead man walking is the feelings and emotions I go through as I try my best to hold on to them as tight as I can without stopping them from being the best versions of themselves. I love my lil' money man, Mitch, my Princess Anylah, my Fat fat Isis, my big baby Sanai, and of course the woman who holds my heart and dreams in her hands, my Chewie Pooh bear, I'm dead without them. I need to show them they are loved and appreciated as much as I can, tomorrow isn't promised, that can't go unsaid. I thought I had more time before with my grandma, my Tay Tay, Lsk and Nakiya, a mistake I will never make again! Every day I'll hold them, kiss them, tell them I love them 😍 nothing will go unsaid, I have to protect them from these feelings I feel. One day soon, I'll see my lost loved ones, maybe that day I'll be whole again. Until then I'll be the best father, husband, friend and son I can be. More importantly I'll be the greatest man I know I can be, no more excuses, no more lies, no more doubts. Greatness is in my reach, in fact it's my birthright so it's a must. When I'm dead and gone that greatness should trickle down to my kids and my queen 👸 ⬛. I'm different, I am not the same, I am damaged, one thing I can do is patch up all the holes that can be repaired and ride this thing called life until the wheels fall off. I'll smile, I'll cry, I'll fight, I'll make improvements, I'll love them relentlessly. I know this is what they need from me.

Life after Death

To my big brother Lsk, aka Rock 5, I never got the chance to express to you the fact that you saved my life. As I went through the toughest time in my life you was there for me and didn't even know it. Your love and unmatched affection saved my life! Literally I was on a path of self-destruction. Wishing we had more time, I never had the opportunity to tell you how much u meant to me, how much I love and appreciate you. Growing up looking up to you, excited to live that rockstar lifestyle like a sponge, I took in everything you taught me and to this day I still value and implement those things in my life. From the woman to the perks lol the baijiu (tiger bone), after-hour spots (frontline), had to come around in my best drip when I was gonna see you, flyest nigga I know. Closing the barbershop late, being the last ones to leave. After hours of bullshitting and watching you hustle! Shit was a beautiful sight to see you amongst the people you loved the most and doing what you loved to do the most. You was truly a god in my eyes, there will never be another you, Rock5! To understand you was to love you, and to know you was an honor, truly a life-changing experience. God only made one rockstar and his names is Lsk - Rock5. I love you, bro, and I miss you like crazy, I still can't believe you're gone, a legend is gone, a father, a brother, a king of kings!!! See you in a min, bro. Your name, your memory will live in my heart forever. Thanks for those days you saved me from myself. I can't wait for the day I'm able to say it to you in person. Save me a spot in your barbershop in the sky!!! I love you the most!!!!!!

Love You the Most

True loyalty doesn't recognize the law. We build together, we heal together, if your body is hurting you can use mine and vice versa. Our loyalty must reign supreme above all else, the impregnable, intimidating passion we possess for one another, it's like no other, itz just different. I can look to her for answers as well as advice, I know when I am wrong she'll check my ass but she knows to do it when it's just us. Our hearts, our minds, our souls are in a place of constant elevation, understanding and compatibility. She can do no wrong, she is my equal as I am hers. No law, no rule, no barriers will ever dictate the position I take with her. I'll side with her every time, any place any time, I am prepared to scorch the universe for her just so she can feel protected and secure. She'll never be lost because my mission is always to find her, she'll always feel love because my mission is to redefine love for her, and she'll always be seen because my job is to capture the beauty of all her flaws and turn them into true art on canvas. I trust her to do the same for me, I trust her to be my universe, I trust her to be my sanctuary, I trust her to be herself and that's loyalty above the law.

Loyalty in the First Degree

Sunflowers and butterflies are what I see when I look at you. Intelligent, beautiful and kind. When I am with you, my mind as well as my heart can only focus on your smile and illuminating energy. I can see the light within you, I can feel the growth going on inside you, it's truly enchanting. Intimate kisses from your forehead down to your collarbone, I enjoy the sweet touch and taste of your lips. I want to hold u tight in my arms, protecting you from everything that's bad in the world in that moment of bliss. You have a smile and a laugh that will bring light to any room, my heart is heavy, my heart is broken, my mind is fractured, I probably need a doctor but I'd rather have my nurse. What nurse is this? one may ask, I respond with a short soliloquy. This is the nurse who has brought light into my days since the day we met, my connection with her is inextricable. She's beautiful and confident, special and unique, humble and pure, this is a brief summary to describe this majestic young queen. My butterfly 🦋 my sunflower 🌻 my nurse 👩 🩺 🩹 .

Nurse Alvarez

The things you try so hard to hide about yourself, are often easily seen. The panic, the anxiety, the sense of failure you feel every moment of every day. You hate yourself for being weak, you hate yourself for letting fear cloud your decisions, you hate yourself for letting down the people who believed in you. You continue to bottle these things up, hoping and praying no one can see right through you, but they can, it's painfully obvious. You can only hold that pain and self-disappointment in but for so long. Not believing in yourself will always show face no matter how hard you hide it, faith will be the deciding factor. Fear and hesitation has made you deviate from your divine path in life. Every day you wake up hoping to die, every day you wake up hoping the pain is gone, every day you wake up praying the fear has left out of your heart. Be cognizant of your worth, being scared, being in pain, having a pinched nerve in your heart is not a crime. You can't hide failure the same way you can't hide success, you can't hide pain the same way you can't hide love and you can't hide fear the same way you can't hide courage. Be mindful of what you choose to hide and what u choose to embrace. You can overcome those insecurities, you can conquer those emotions, fear is not real, it's a choice not a reality. Never deviate from your path, no matter what's put in your way. Courage under fire will always keep your soul satisfied, keep u on your toes. Once you embrace that narrative, you'll never have to hide again.

Secret Squirrel

Only one person can truly have your heart and soul as well as your mind and body. You'll give everything in your heart without question, without fear of heartbreak to your one true love. This person is a magnificent creature inside and out. Majestic and pure, the light in all of the dark spaces in your life. Humility, loyal, beautiful, and smart. Courageous as well as kind hearted, her true strength being her mind and her weakness being her heart. It's important that we covet our black women as well as protect them with our lives, black man. Think of everything we could accomplish, she's a rockstar, she's my rock and I her King. 👑 📿 🎤

Short and Sweet

Treat every moment as if it has the potential for magic. Long nights and even longer days, practice patience and illuminate each moment that puts a dent in your heart and a smile on your face. It's easy to create chaos, it's simple to destroy something versus putting together a self-proclaimed legacy. The dreams, the aspirations, the obsessive need to be great, lives in us. This we are reminded of each time we close our eyes and sleep at night, they make random popups in our heads, like a flashback from last night as we daydream, in search for our life paths. Silence is full of mystery and assumptions, noise is full of anxiety and destruction, life is full of hard lessons, good and bad. You are full of life, you can give it and you can take it, the decision is yours and no one else's. I often ask myself three simple questions, one being, How will I be remembered? Can I achieve my goals despite the mental pressures, as well as the financial barriers I face as a black man in white America? Will my people have raise together in beautiful harmony and take back what's rightfully ours, the world and everything in it!? What are the questions that keep you up at night? What are the answers to the questions that keep you fighting? When it's all said and done, will those questions be answered? Will you be satisfied with the effort you put forth? Only time will tell, for now ask the most important question, what can you do now?

Balance

It's only cheating if the rules have merit. It's only betrayal if you care. It's only injustice when you're any other race than black. It's not murder if they deserved it. It doesn't hurt if you don't scream. It's not depression if you're smiling and laughing. It's not hate if you don't say it out loud. It's not domestic violence if "they made you do it." It's not rape if she was wearing provocative clothing. It's not an addiction if you can function. It's only snitching if you tell on your friends/family. It's not lying if you don't get caught. It's not valid unless the masses agree. If you're not a leader you are a follower, stop making excuses and make progress. Redefine love, reinvent life, throw away that primitive low vibration way of thinking. Be a real one, don't be a coward. It's only a dream if you have a plan. It's only you if there is no me.

The Black Plague

Vengeance is a lazy form of grief. Existence is chaos, under the surface of every black man is a deep hope to be Loved and respected by the black woman. The fear of being viewed as inadequate, replaceable, or obsolete is a truly demoralizing feeling. I love the black woman, I believe her place in this world is next to the Blackman. Who else can fully understand the divinity, love, strength and passion we possess outside of the black woman? Who else can we feel comfortable with as we are crying out for help, "Hold us, queens, hold us, my beautiful black goddess." These are real tears of pain and generational frustrations. We have to be insanely strong in this world that views us as feeling like monsters, broken, unhealed, with no sense of intuition, or empathy. Just another nigga that could be killed like a dog in the street and, just another nigga the world can use and abuse until it's time to throw them to the side. At the end of the day we need our Black women just as much as they need us, the two can never reach their full potential without one another. Black love, the black family is the real holy trinity, the black man, the black woman and the black child, immortality in human form. I can't wait to the day where we will stand strong and unified as we begin to love us, love one another, and actually take some pride in the gift of being black. Teach, love, and comfort the ones who look like you, it's the natural order of things. No more letting the European views of love and family dictate how we live our lives and how we love one another. White supremacy will no longer conquer the minds of our people. Live black, love black, heal within and then heal outwards. Protect the black family, protect the black traditions and more importantly build the youth to be better and stronger than we are now. No more self-hate. No more black men and black women going against each other, as they amalgamate with an outside race over their own. Be proud of who u are and who you will be as a whole, living free, loving black, and die with peace and love knowing that you spent your life with the only one for you. Holding us, loving us, understanding us, is a space only reserved for the Black women period. Black women, take your place on the throne. Black men only.

The Holy Trinity

In life you never know which moments will be memorable. Live every moment memorably, no matter how significant you may view it at the moment. The beautiful thing about life is the unexpected people, things and places we cross paths with as it's downloaded and stored into our temporal lobes (the hippocampus) and transformed into long-term memories in the brain's cortex. Without even thinking about it we can journey back to those moments that provided us with a joyful smile when we are in the middle of having a bad day, we can feel the sun hitting our faces on a cold and rainy day, we can feel the kiss of a love one without having them in arm's reach. Memories have a funny way of shaping our lives, often times in a peculiar way, it comes out of nowhere like a deer in headlights and throws you off balance into a salubrious state of bliss. Often times we neglect all the positives in our life as we drown ourselves in the negative, this is a mistake, really it's an outrage. Why covet the dark when you can control the light? Treat even the less significant moment like it could be "a day for the books," treat the people you come in contact with as if they will be the last person to see you, give them a moment worth remembering. Visit the places you've deemed your happy place and share it with someone in need, we have the ability to pass on memories from one person to the next, from one place to another and back into our temporal lube. Happiness, tranquility, serenity, peace all tied into our minds, bodies, and souls, causing a chain reaction of outer body freedom. Less negativity, more positivity and more importantly enjoy the beautiful freedoms of your mind, feel free to pass them along.

The Vault

My soul is dissatisfied, my heart is broken and my mind is on the brink of a colossal meltdown. My vision is impaired, my sense of direction is constantly rerouting, go left, go right, make a U-turn. I take a second to try and understand why is everything goin' so wrong, what's the endgame here, am I just here to be stepped over and devalued by the ones I trust and call loved ones? Is the universe out to get me? Shit, did I do something wrong and maybe didn't realize it? These are a few questions that must be asked as well as answered. The feeling of inadequacy raining on me like a ton of bricks, I am dodging bricks like Muhammad Ali dodging punches. Float like a butterfly and sting like a bee, I finally understand that he wasn't taking about his opponent in the ring. In fact, it's about the opponents you face in life and having the ability to float like a butterfly to achieve the highs of your dreams and to sting like a bee to protect yourself from the things and people who want to harm us. A classic boxing analogy transformed from a flamboyant statement into a way of life. Magnanimous, dastardly, episodic, audacious, ambiguous, like a black panther in the wintertime, I am both diminished and dangerous. Keep your guard up and never forget to float.

Virtuoso

The obvious isn't always visible. Some things are put in our path to challenge us as well as transform us in to better souls. Struggle and frustration vs. wealth and privilege. No matter the path picked for you, there will be good times and bad times, there will be happy and joyful times as well devastating anomalies. You must find comfort in yourself as you look towards the future, with an open mind as well as a steady heart. It's time to be prepare as you navigate your way to the goals and aspirations you hope to achieve no matter what, good, bad, together or alone, get it done. Focusing on the future and still having to focusing on what's right in front of you will not be an easy feat. Self-reflection, self-worth, self-courage, these internal intangibles will help assist you through certain trials and tribulations. No matter which situation you are currently in struggle or wealth, happy or sad, don't give up no matter the cost. Keep striving for the best, keep your head up and keep your heart pure. I've lost myself a thousand times, it's truly a mystery how I am still able to function and continue to live life. Shit hurts like a third-degree burn, only time can heal the pain and hurt. Live life, have fun but be responsible with yourself and your loved ones. Life is to short and once it's over, it's over, no do-overs, no second chances, just one life full of multiple situations, multiple close friends and loved ones, enemies and haters. At the end of the day it's only one you, living your one life. Discover the best version of yourself that you can find, that's all anyone can ask for.

What if I Could See My Future

The Journey as just begun….to be continued…

Printed in the USA
CPSIA information can be obtained
at www.ICGtesting.com
JSHW040458051223
52793JS00005B/41

9 780916 307448